Strange What Rises

Also by Gary J. Whitehead

A Glossary of Chickens
Measuring Cubits While the Thunder Claps
The Velocity of Dust

Strange What Rises

Gary J. Whitehead

Terrapin Books

Terrapin Books
4 Midvale Avenue
West Caldwell, NJ 07006

www.terrapinbooks.com

ISBN: 978-1-947896-13-0
LCCN: 2018964642

First Edition

Cover art: "Lake of Ice"
by Jace Knie
www.jaceknie.com

for Betsy

Contents

Wild Columbine

Some bells ring of their own accord.
Some need the boy who pulls the rope
and is lifted off his feet on the upswing.
The pigeons scatter from the tower's
shaken air. Their paratrooper feathers
storm the shaft of light. By what
miracle does he recall, years later,
such ascension, the last time he loved
a church, was lifted, literally, by song?
These wild columbines are bells
that will never be rung
save by hummingbirds and bees,
drunk on their nectar,
having no knowledge of their reviled name.
Will we ever love that word again?
The heart claps at the sound of it,
but no sound comes, only the flowers
swinging on their stems to lift me,
feet planted like those of the hangman
who watches the hanged man kick the air.

Pretend It Was Just the Wind

Water crept into our furnished home,
the one in the flood zone but zoned
anyway, and anyway our home,

though we spent so little time there.
And now that we've moved on,
I think of the outlets sparking out

and my guitar rising against the wall
until it fell and became a boat
that drifted from room to room,

knocking into legs of tables and chairs.
I think of the books the water took
from the shelves and opened

at its leisure as it snaked and rose,
the rain still rapping at the roof
and at the swollen windows.

And of all the items of our life—
our braided rugs, the dog's bed
and bowls, the sofa with its pillows,

the lamps, the photos, the figurines—
all of them out of their element and into another,
which held them and rocked them gently.

The Weight

Heavier than I would have thought,
heavier than a sack of flour,
than a bag of Vidalias or, better yet,

a meshed bunch of oranges,
she smelled vaguely of baby powder
and milky spit. Yes, she was heavy,

and my arms, after five minutes,
hurt, but I held her anyway,
heavy as she was,

and Laurence, her mother,
said I had a way though I didn't
think I did and still don't. And now

I can't remember the baby's name
or how I came to be staying
at that lake house in the first place,

or why I might have taken
that child in my arms, that weight,
that gummy, smiling face

and those chubby, kicking legs.
But I remember she was heavy
and that I was glad to pass her back,

sweet as she was but that
I couldn't stop staring
into those tiny, gray eyes,

which seemed to see
something in me
once there was nothing left

to hold but my aching.

Farmhouse

So, wooden heart,
with your painted chambers
and your warped floors,
how have you been without me?
I left, as it were, no windows
open, their lead weights
suspended in the dark
by old rope sashes.
Now I've come after so long gone
as if to whom I was yesterday,
my close, my humble home,
my old familiar,
and the lamps I left on
still burn in their glass sconces.
Will you love the new me
as I love the old you,
your attic massacres
of stinging things,
your treacherous cellar passage?
Still the weepy sink,
the mousy counter,
the strike-anywhere matches.
I see the butcher knives still cling
to the needy magnet.
Same ceiling stain,
rust-colored,
like evaporated blood.
I'm sorry for the black banana
in the too-big bowl.
I'm sorry for the grate full of ashes.

Let me raise the storms.
After so long gone this house
still looks like mine,
but it smells like someone else's.

Rough Terrain

In the bug-infested forest
of my many regrets,
I step from the marked path—
the house and the marriage
and the baby carriage—
and stumble into overgrown brambles
and strangling vines
thick with black flies and gnats.
I slap, and the steaming forest
of my many regrets
slaps back. It throws up
one muscled root
on which I stub and trip,
dropping things as I go
that I might come again
under a shaded canopy
and catch my breath
in the bug-infested forest
of little deaths.
I can hear the birdsong
below the ferns,
the hermit thrush I know I am,
full-throated flute of the ferns
echoing solitude
through deadfalls
and green clearings
where gilled children
lift cups of curdled cream.
So much so poisonous.
So much that stings.
Mud daubers and wasps,

fire ants and chiggers and ticks.
Horsefly of regret,
mosquito of regret
ever at my ears
in this infested forest,
where does the hermit sing
when the seething ends
and the frosts begin?
Will I struggle still
with my cool blue call
through the forest of my shame?
A woodsman told me once
that winter is the ideal time
to travel over rough terrain.

Because It Is Cold and Nightfall Comes

In the cave of the chest the wild heart drums
around a fire and clutches close a fur
because it is cold and nightfall comes.

In that wilderness the cold wind numbs
everything it touches, so we take cover
in the cave of the chest. The wild heart drums

on stretched skin. And someone else strums
the stringed instrument inside of her
because it is cold and nightfall comes.

The fire-lit walls, whatever they become,
become things we never thought they were.
In the cave of the chest the wild heart drums,

but the drums have never felt palms or thumbs
or fists, never throbbed in the open air
because it is cold and nightfall comes.

Call it what you will, the chamber hums.
Fear-sack, lonely hold, old music maker.
In the cave of the chest the wild heart drums
because it is cold and nightfall comes.

Moose in the Yard

It came like a dark thing done,
ambling out of a thicket,
sniffing the swing set and slide.

It came with its long, phallic face
and its open pillory of antlers
velvety as cat-o'-nines.

It ate the yew. It ate the hostas.
It kept me hostage in the house
of dark things done,

for as sweet as it looked
lying in the crabgrass and clover
(and eating those, too),

I knew it was an animal, wild,
capable of great violence
and weighing way more

than a dark thing done,
being muscle and bone, tooth
and hoof, and not immaterial

or justifiable. When it rose,
startled by the security light,
a bit weak in the knees,

or so it seemed, I thought
for a second of the way
I must look getting up

from our post-hoc slumber,
languid and still a little taut
from sleep. It ate the day

lilies. It ate my whiskey
barrel herbs. It stepped into a shadow
like a dark thing done,

and then it was at the window,
where the thistle seed hung,
and it gazed back at me, blinking.

Garden Shed in Winter

It was unfazed by cold. In fact, it seemed
content with disuse. The rolled packs of seeds,
the bamboo poles and tomato cages.
The oil-stained floor and clods of dried grass.
I hadn't touched anything since the fall,
when it was all I could do to keep from
rakes and tarps, tulip bulbs with their pom-pom
roots. The fly inside gave sense to it all.
Now I was there, wondering why I'd come.
The shovels leaned where I'd left them.
The spade and hoe. The twine hung from its peg.
There, a pea-sized mummy rolled in a web.
Couldn't I see there was nothing to do?
I took a last look and pulled the door to.

Cleromancy

In laps, on stoops, in plots of dust,
with stones, with sticks, with chunks of dung,
they cast their lots and found

in what was flung the means
they needed. One lot for the Lord,
one for the goat with the spotted head.

Let loose in a wilderness, it heard
the wind of its brother's bloodlet end,
paused, and rolled its cud. With cuds,

with knuckles, with gems (the Urim
and Thummim), yes, with whatever
instruments God gave them,

as long as volition, in its division,
dropped from cupped hands and left them
blameless as eggless nests.

With eggs, with wood, with pebbles,
on tables, in fields, on decks of ships,
they cast their lots, wanting what I want—

to decide without deciding,
to find some guidance, to take up,
like divided garments, the will

of God and try it on for size.
The dice I roll, the coin I flip,
the thoughts that drop in my mind

like twigs and which I analyze.
Life choices I hold in my hand,
lengths hidden by the fist of fate.

Child I never had—O Jonah
thrown over! Equivocal calm.
In scrimshaw I might have carved out

your life had I not strewn the shards,
the little bones, the dried beans,
had I been a better shepherd.

The Bearded Slave

In the gallery, I shuffled among
the hushed crowd, our footfalls
a kind of song, the magic we held

flashing and flashing
as we circled the Prigioni, stone-dead
but larger than the lives we lived.

Unfinished. Unyielding. Immovable.
How I sometimes feel,
waiting in the slab of my life,

metamorphic, veined, swirled
with impurities—silt of the sad,
chert of the venal, clay of the remorseful me.

A slave to the rock-hard days ahead,
which flash and gleam as they come,
and my form in there God knows where.

Out in the piazza, a horse clopped past,
iron-shod, ringing. Someone coughed.
A pigeon flapped. Dust bloomed

in the slant of the window's light.
Mallet in one hand, chisel in the other,
an eyelash in his right eye, Michael,

more than a mortal, Angel divine,
paused, wiped, then struck again. Why, when I saw the prisoners,

couldn't I free them, my hand drawn
to the marble I couldn't touch?
I could only imagine their struggle,

so strange under the watchful eye of David,
who stood godlike and complete,
haughty in his perfection, free,

as if he might step from his pedestal
and walk toward a brook to look for stones.

The Wall

There, they—in their blue-dawning day,
with hammers and chisels and sledges,

on either side—pummeled the cold stone,
sang songs, called in their shared tongue,

while we, across an ocean, shared tongue
and paused every now and then

to watch through fogged glass and barbed wire
the jumbo jets charge, lift, loom

above my hot, parked car,
drown out The Clash and leave a ringing.

Our skin graffitied by shadows and the red-lit dash.
Our kisses, I see now, just puffs of dust.

Her on me, seat back. Our teeth clacked.
The wall. By then they'd broken through.

Eye to eye at the mouth of a glorious revolution.
And I? I pounded away with what little I had

as my small world shook with an arrival.

Grounded

You who would fly into the day-
chasing night, there's no room left for you.

The late-night bars have closed early, too.
Can you see the jets in their descent?

They come in a queue like stars
that follow the rule of some new universe,

down and down, till tires meet tarmac
with a screech, a sigh of smoke.

Can you hear the light-rail train?
It needs so much to stay on track

it flattens the coins the child parted with
just to feel such a thing.

What else holds on? What else
must touch down, refuel?

All manner of vehicle.
The migrating tern, the warbler

that can't keep still. The stomach
demands it as the branch demands it,

as the ground demands the oak
stand in the yard all its life,

as the seabed demands the sea,
the earth everything to its center,

where there is no room either
though it holds everything close.

The Falling Man

In the most
known photo
he looks just
like a
diver—
mid-descent, the
steel his sea—so
slowly he
seems to
fall, one
black leg
bent as in that
other kind of
dive (a can opener
I think they
call it), but
his a dive from the
burning
tower of his
life, from
Windows on the
World,
leaving this
world from the
ledge of
his assured
death.
What
the lesser known
photographs show

is the wind
stripping him
of his bright white shirt,
the talons of that
eagle-eyed
mid-morning air tearing
at his salmon tee,
and not really grace,
not really quietude
at all
but a flailing plunge,
a loss of control
in the last act
he could control,
which was to leap
from the relative safety
of that high floor, hot
as it was
and smoke-choked,
into the unsolid air,
which might be
like heaven
but fleet
and palpable
and there
for all of us to see
and—for those
who were
there—
to hear.

A Flock of Starlings

What dark thoughts gather in these trees,
every bit of news seizing the fleeing light
to roost above the park and blather,

the bare branches suddenly leafed
in black and raining uric acid.
I clap once, and everything ceases,

that second when nothing is heard
but wings, and the stripped trees shiver.
First toward the river, then toward town,

up and then down, and back this way
again, the murmuration wends as one,
until it's all bad news, a specter

in the sky, the horizon's black ballet.
The velvet slides along its track.
I call the dog and turn toward home.

Shoring Up

Houses half in shadow, half in rising sun,
and, nearby, a flag whipping ocean breeze.
A man with headphones on his morning run.
Car wheels backing over gravel. These,

and a crow cawing from a stunted pine,
a gull on an updraft, the hiss of the sea.
I've woken again to a porch not mine,
free from toil, free from calamity.

These, and a thousand other sufferings.
I sit at the table and fill my bowl.
Seabirds cackle viciously. The wind rings
a counterweight against a metal pole.

A Shiver of Sharks

Seen from the drone, they looked like sperm
aswim in a green-lit womb,
serene yet greedy,

and the Chris-Craft the ovum swarmed.
Everything, at a distance,
goads to be contradicted.

The slaveship-speck spied through a spyglass
bobbing under its white sails,
its horrors unheard.

With its basement torture chamber,
the farmhouse lying quaintly
in a quilted landscape

seen briefly from a passing plane.
The avalanche, volcano,
twister from afar.

But up close, too, the image lies.
Cancer, through a microscope,
looks like a Pollock

or something cosmic—galaxies,
nebulas, flares glimpsed through Chandra.
How artfully

we see, how glibly we gainsay.
More so these eye-in-the-sky days.
Meanwhile the mackerel

in their schools at the upwellings.
And the sharks, whose eyes, aside
from their retinas,

are not unlike our own.

Loons

Up to the black and light-riddled surface,
they rise, shaking
out of nowhere, as memories
do from their depths, uninvited, merciless
and buoyant with uncertainties.

Tonight, seeing one noiselessly appear
in the breaking
lines of a full moon's bright writing,
yards from the dock, I remembered your hair
on a night when we were fighting.

So much of it had fallen out by then.
You were taking
strands of it and strangling your thumb.
Strange what rises, red-eyed and unbidden,
with a beauty that strikes us dumb.

Cordon Sanitaire

Inside, there is ague, fever,
something like a whisper
passing from mouth to mouth

and ear to ear, the germ of an idea
creeping through mangroves
and strands of oil palms,

staggering into wattle-and-daub huts
and corrugated shacks,
into neural folds and cortex.

Outside, there are armed guards,
a day-night sentry of worries.
No one allowed in or out.

Centuries-old, this practice.
Leper colonies on mountaintops,
disfigurements shuffling in thin air.

In Venetian harbors
ships lay at anchor for forty days
before plague-free merchants

could row toward shores
with their sacks of spices
and piles of bright silks.

In St. Petersburg
the tsar's troops
pointed their swords at cholera.

In the purple Pyrenees
an army assembled,
fifteen-thousand strong,

because of a single germ
carried across the sea
in a Cuban brick.

And so, too, in the equatorial now:
out there, the nothingness
of night and jeering guns;

and in here, the black shapes
struggling for their lives
and held in by imaginary lines.

Purgatory Chasm

Now I spelunk through time,
thinking my way between heaves
of doubt, feeling
in the dark for passages
and hints of diffuse illumination,
less sure than when, as a boy,
I slid headfirst into that womb
of glacial confusion,
probing with a diminishing
beam slick seams and strange
formations—Corn Crib
and Coffin, Pulpit
and Fat Man's Misery.
The point then was to slink
as deep as I might, lose myself
in dead ends and sharp enjambments
until, too tired to move,
penlight dead, I'd lie panting
and panicked in cool blindness
like a wounded mole.
Was this the purgatory
I'd been taught in school,
postmortem layover?
Sandwiched in granite,
I loved the not-knowing,
and I still do—the crawl forward,
word after word,
the glimmer on the rockface,

and, finally, the way out
and the white so bright
that my eyes, without
my wanting, must close.

Toward the Far Shore

Blind, long-tailed, albino koi, my little swimmers
swim intrepid in the dark, swim the warm pond
of my reclining love. Drained, we lie entwined

while the encoded fishes swim, my brain balanced
on the edge of sleep, where a painter has erected
his paint-spattered easel, and midges swarm,

and the koi rise to nibble. The fish-kissed surface
forms rings as if from drizzle. Pendent willows
brush the bank the way your hair swept my face

when we raced to the finish. Toward the far shore
a frog drags its carpet bag of spawn. Below our
window, a minivan chirps, its doors thunk closed,

its engine chuffs to life, and its tires seethe
on the rain-soaked road. So the real swims in,
feckless. Comings and goings. Afternoon

of the now and nothing-doing of the aging us,
spent and infecund, our encircled life
growing wider still in the stillness.

The Red Eft

What were you doing in the path
of my life, infant of the sun,
newt of my sometime compunction?

As if nothing could spot you.
As if you'd never been spotted,
splayed, five-fingered and five-toed.

Not even my prodding with a stick,
not even my fifties, my fathering weakness
for terrestrials could compel you.

Behind us on the trail a girl
called to her father. Or was it a boy?
Or were they ahead of us,

who'd taken a wrong turn by then
and would be late for checkout
back at the quaint hotel?

Flying Saucers

Some regrets take the air,
almost visibly, bright
against the mind's wide sky.
The child you never had,
for some reason red-haired.
The way you said goodbye
to your first real girlfriend.

The boy, the bicycle,
the stop sign you ignored.
Staying on vacation
despite your father's stroke,
your mother's failing heart.
Chips on red and not black.
The phone call you refused

to pick up from your friend
stopped on a bridge, car door
flung open. Deleting
his voicemail. Not even
listening. They're out there
somewhere—qualms, misgivings,
just waiting to be launched

the way those clay pigeons did
when I went skeet shooting
with David, who saved me,
to whom I've not spoken
in a decade. Regrets
I want to blow to bits,
like those orange clay disks

when I led correctly,
timing blast with arc
so that each Day-Glo plate
pulverized in mid-air
into the dust from which
it originated.

Returning to Iowa

Above the just cut field
martins darted through the dusty air,
diminishing astonishingly
the swarms of gnats and moths
orbiting the great round bales,
which sat in their warm compactness
like cakes on racks.
Shadows grinned on the unsunned sides,
and I remember us happy
in a Midwestern way, stretched out
and drowsy, a stop on a trip
to Amana, your hand warm and wet in mine.
A kestrel hovered above the ditch.
A mile off, a pickup made a gray wake
along a gravel road.
A cow crested a hill
and paused to contemplate us.
Some things are not countable in their grace,
so we pine for them,
we remember them with kindness,
we return them to the mouth
to chew them a second time.

Old Loves

They wait in the dark, as in drawers,
like matches grabbed from restaurants,
their addresses, their phone numbers
forgotten. Maybe the power's
out. Maybe we've funked up a room.
Or we're bored. So we take them out.
We strike them for the flame they make.
We shake them for their forgiving smoke.

Husbandry

Our love in a topple
like slabs of quarried marble,

though I saw a polished house.

Grass grew around it, poison
sumac and ivy, trees of heaven,

though I saw Italian gardens.

A cacophony of birds—finches
and flickers, thrushes and jays,

one red-bellied woodpecker

who hammered our rotting soffit,
but I heard an avian choir,

days with repeating phrases,

whole summers of arias.
Rings around my eyes from

the opera glasses. Robin alarms,

but you were there beside me.
Towers tumbled then.

Whole cities exploded.

The ark sank with its animals
two-by-two. Why couldn't I see

the people leaping, the boy

washed up on that foreign shore?
What tyrant was I to hold

the plan for world dominion

in one hand and some seeds
in the other for the exhausted dove?

Fly in Our Salad

The sweet greens we spun—the baby
kale and baby chard, beet greens
also in their infancy, oak leaf lettuce
in two varieties, littlest shoots
of arugula—and the last red onion
from the skin-littered bin,
the grape tomatoes and gherkins.
All of it so tender so early in spring,
everything eager to grow,
and the two of us eager to eat them
dressed in a mustard vinaigrette
and plated at the outside table.
Good china and white cloth napkins.
Your wine breathing in its glass.
And just as we toasted the season
with a clink, there arrived a fat, black fly,
which licked its chops and gazed
at us and winked its many eyes.

Destroying Angel

Little basilicas have formed on the lawn,
pure white stipes and caps like separated cream,
places to congregate for ants and gnats.

Conjured by a storm, born out of warm ground,
they just as soon turn sad, blacken and sag,
their fruited bodies roofed with slime.

Up the spiral staircase and down again
plod the soldiers of God. And here I am
ruminating on the comely and the poisonous,

plucking them this religious afternoon,
gall for gall, in the way of all destroying angels,
whom only time can rebuke or chasten.

Horace, I Dream of Watches

windowed thick with sapphire crystals and alive
with hands that sweep around exquisite faces
set in gold or stainless steel cases.

I dream the dream of futile calculations—
the time in Rome or Delhi nocked on gemmy bezels,
the keeping more reliable than ghazals.

Lugs and crowns, escapements and Geneva Seals,
the boaty rotor rocking in a jeweled sea—
these through a skeleton back I see,

like my own bones, my own heart ticking on reserve
until there's nothing left to dress for. Please,
when the main spring's sprung and the gears all seize,

let there be more than Jove's winters to give.
Time may keep. I'll keep time while I live.

Making Love in the Kitchen

We do it with knives in hand,
blue tongues licking the bottoms of pots,
steam fogging the windows from hearts
of artichokes being strained.

Hearts are made to be carved
out, cooked soft, slathered with butter,
fork-stabbed and lifted to another's
open mouth. We say we are starved,

as though we were doing this alone,
lonely as an onion in its skin,
say we are starving when what we mean
is that we want to postpone

the inevitable, which is inedible,
however we dice
it, and so we make—as it consumes us—
this love we call a meal.

Parting Ways

All at once you're out of love again,
and it's like the earth has jerked on its axis,

and the screen door slaps shut behind you,
and you cross a meadow and enter

the woods, one branch swinging like the door
to a saloon, and soon you're in a clearing

where a hunter crouches over a body
you smelled long before you got there.

A suicide, he says, and there's a note.
The skin yellow, preserved by some concoction—

antifreeze and orange juice—so the buzzards
and bears, the foxes and coyotes and coons

would eschew it. The bottle still in his hand.
The eyes like those tiny, translucent onions

you find at the bottom of a jar of pickles.
But what sickens the most is a week later

the hunter's dating the dead guy's ex,
and you clink bottles at the bar when he tells of it.

Snow Buntings

That they come at all,
these late fall insistencies,

that they should flit
within me, lifting

and settling at a distance,
as if my fifties were

that meadow I meandered
and my untried time that flock

I scared up the day
the first snow came,

buntings white and russet,
buntings I hadn't yet seen

and so far south
my companion

said it was unusual;
that they come at all,

these mid-life glimpses,
as of the windblown seeds

in the stone dust road,
seeds the buntings returned to,

lifting and settling at a distance;
that they come at all,

especially late
in the fall before the white

of snow and ice,
surprises me less than that

I welcome them, that I can
imagine myself reluctant

to leave the earth,
wanting still to eat of it,

but forced to fly by the approach
of something dark and larger.

When My Love Gave Chase

A black thing scrabbled
high in a pine by the pond,
and my love, swimming
there, heard it and made
for shore, dragging the pond
with him. The beast bore down,
a shadow as unformed
as what today
we term tomorrow,
and my sweet boy ran
toward it, trailing water
like a brown cape.
Countless rough-skinned newts,
poised in their toxin,
bellyflopped. Then all
was a blur and a decade.
All still but the dragonflies
struggling out of their cracklings,
the hollow claws of which
clutched the blades
of the highest grasses.
I wait most of his life
and he appears at the bend
in the dusty road,
unscathed but panting,
his pink tongue
as long as a bear's
and dripping spit like honey.

He leaps, as always,
through the passenger door,
shameless and almost glad,
towheaded, brown-eyed
son I never had.

Coronation

I'll never know the rupture and the gush,
the crown, or the crowning, the gummy grin
of the vulva, hair for teeth, the soft orb
forced forth without volition, the pungent room,
king mushroom wrenched from its mycelium.

Or parade or pageantry or one-car
motorcade. Or skid knee or broken bone.
Or gold star, or silver, face on the fridge.
Or the balled loss—like a runaway pearl—
of the one gone before his time. Or hers.

A loss like theirs, who entered the chapel
in the litter of their reciprocal grief
while their son's song wound down to its end
and we all looked on as some of us had
years before, at his baptism, the deacon

dipping his head into the marble font,
his tiny crown anointed—as kings, priests,
and prophets are except with sacred oil.
What a small solace to know I'd never
feel such grief, I must have thought on the route

back to our empty house, steering through
the city's slush, crossing over the steel
bridge, and heading back up the palisades,
alongside which the brackish river flowed
like a gilded carpet toward the sea.

Gray Water

Gray water of the wayward
    and third-world, the weary
traveler out of underwear,

    the off-grid anchorite I was
standing naked by a basin,
    up to my elbows in it.

Gray water of the great unwashed,
    bare hands wringing,
cloths bleeding into buckets

    like gutted birds. The Gambia's,
the Ganges' turbid water
    slopping out of pails.

My grandmother's
    when she laundered by hand
in spite of a machine.

    Gray water of every
washerwoman's walk
    to and from a well.

Middle fork of the South Platte,
    the Otoe woman on her knees, leaking
a white soldier's semen.

    Her gray water. Her red
hands squeezing,
    and on the far bank,

the whole scene curved
        in the brown eye of a bison
chewing its cud.

        Gray-red water of a butchered
fawn in a hunter's
        backwoods tub.

The Yellowstone's,
        the Gila's boiled water gone gray
with pioneer grime.

        The Choctaw's, the Chickasaw's
gray water. The Mississippi's,
        full of silt, in which the Ojibwas

bathed their blankets
        and Twain's maid rinsed ink
from his stained linens.

        The Niger's, the Mekong's,
the Volga's dreggy water
        pulled clean down highlands

and glacial plateaus to lave lace,
        jacquard, ankara, to scrub filth
out of shawl and yem.

        Gray water of every river,
lake and stream, the sinners'
        tributaries, the masturbators',

no agitators or paddles.
How easy to straddle a pail, decoct
a murder from a shirt,

to twist from sheets the shame
of menstruation,
the wetted bed,

our shit and cum.
To mundify, to deterge.
From the gray water

of our fey humanity,
from the dust, smut,
and crud, we pull dripping

the piece goods of our deeds.
A little elbow grease, a little soap,
a little water cleans us.

O, Trout

My manhood's muscled brother,
my frowning other,
your death is a river I return to
like a lover whose love drowned there
and now the whole village,
once a year, launches
a flotilla of glowing boats.
How would my sadness,
hidden on a hook, look to you?
I keep it still in a Styrofoam box
where it wraps around
my other sadnesses
and probes the dark loam
for its release.
Meanwhile the river.
Meanwhile the sea.
Upriver no one has heard
of the one night in April
when the caravan's lanterns
pass along the wet road.
Downriver a tavern
has been erected in your name.
I stop there sometimes
when the river is high
with winter melt
and sip at life by the fire.
Forgive the barb.
Forgive the needle-nose pliers.
I tried to revive you.

I've tried to live as you,
facing the current,
seeking the least resistance,
watching the shimmering flotsam
between me and what can't be breathed.

Sensible Transfer

Winter forms its
slow occlusions
like lake-made icicles
on each lapping wave-
splashed tuft or frond,
a drop at a time,
till the shoreline grows
teeth that seem to chatter,
seem to chew,
with their changing
states of matter,
the insistent spray.
Don't such strange formations
take their shapes in us, too?
Our *eyes* ice over,
our nails lengthen
into claws despite
how we trim them,
our hate-made teeth
bite what caresses us.
In a matter of weeks
the whole body
might be made
one solid mass
that moans and cracks
in its shifting, something
that now can be trod on,
thick as it is, though
slippery and cold to touch.
In time, it pulls

from the shore,
the dark, limbal ring
widening around the lens
of cataracted ice
until it's an island,
then a tiny
berg
bobbing in the middle,
and then,
as though forgiven,
it's just a lake again.

Reservoir

So cold we made bonfires on the ice,
the hair beneath our caps as gray as the day,
which was as gray as the ice but streaming
low-slung light. Some of us in skates
that wrote the hours we moved through,
a score for two pianos or the pendent branches
that shook their glass chimes when the northerlies blew.
The lake, too, with its boom and whistle,
its lightning cracks we chased to the shrinking edge
where the water rocked dark against the shore.
More light! Why should one brief day
typify a life? Looking back, I remember
looking back. At the eyes of our fires blinking.
At the sun sinking into bare, black trees.

Heat Lightning

—for Alyne "Lady" Buder
July 22, 1928-December 26, 2012

The whole drive home it split the swart-browed sky
like the forked veins of my forehead—
root rents, rhizomes
of light

and associations. Clouds of musings
now—why I'm reminded of rains
I wished would come
and mute

flashes of brilliance in a blue distance.
Late that afternoon we'd released
purple balloons
that rose

almost spookily toward a rainbow.
Someone said it was Lady.
A nephew asked me
questions

for which I had no responses. Can we
see rainbows up close? Is there life
after death? How
high would

they rise and where and when might they touch down?
I thought of a boy happening
upon one in
a field,

a half-deflated, wrinkled mass trailing
a lavender ribbon. Were they
up there? I asked
myself

on the drive. Were they dodging the crackling
of the atmosphere, or had they
already gone
higher,

rising like the human idea, which flashes
even as one steers between
the lines toward
home?

Driving All Night

First, there are the songs on the stations you love
and the two of you dancing in your seats,
thumbs keeping time on the wheel,
windows half-way down, the sun sinking
in the distance, and the city a gray, fading,
jagged line dividing the rearview mirror.
Then, the traffic thins, the smog clears,
the stations you love fizzle into static
and you switch to CDs, then MP3s.
Brake lights, two by two, veer off redly
to the right until, over the next hill,
nothing rolls before you but the yellow lines
in the short-sightedness of your low beams.
Now the smell of farms—alfalfa and hay,
cow pies and corn—and beyond the wind
of the cracked windows and moonroof
a seething of crickets and katydids.
Your lover asleep in the reclined seat,
you switch off the stereo and tune in
to the hum of the road, the rattle somewhere
in the dash, the flash and gale of a passing
tractor-trailer. You watch needle and gauge,
scan signs for rest stops or gas. You pinch
at crumbs of pretzels or chips in a greasy bag,
swig the last of the water. Miles and miles,
your head growing heavy, your back
beginning to ache, your plans second-guessed
or altogether regretted, a pumping like pistons
in your empty gut. What but the hoped-for

pinkening in the east to think of, then,
you who are driving, you who are driven
through the night, which is dark and long?

Summer Leaves

Headlights snaked
through hemlocks
and black pines,

not in any hurry,
though not without
a sense of seeking,

one lamp tilted up
toward the trees,
where something

seemed to hide,
the other staring
straight ahead

and now into the green,
shining disks
of a mule deer's eyes,

which, when the beam passed,
blinked a few times
and saw, perhaps,

the fatigued faces
at the station wagon's windows
and then the dusty trailer

behind. Maybe the deer
watched as the car
creaked to a stop

and the people stepped out,
hungry and a little stiff,
the father backing the camper

into a level spot,
the mother lighting a lantern,
her children huddling

in its yellow glow.
Maybe the deer was a doe,
and, in the safety of the dark,

she nudged her spotted fawns
and went on chewing
the sweet summer leaves.

Forgetfulness

What she can't remember comes apart
in me so that my heart confuses its rooms.

She irons, and the crease uncreases,
the steam hisses, her washed thoughts

call up ancient vacations—a laundromat
in Maine, the four of us shivering naked

while the machines churned our grime,
the time we caught blue crabs on the Cape,

our trunks black with inlet mud.
But she can't remember what she's just said.

There's a freshness to forgetfulness.
And when there is no more memory,

everything will be clean and put away.
She pulls another shirt from the basket.

I wander the rooms where I grew,
rooms soon to be someone else's.

I feel the embossed spines of old book sets,
their wrinkled titles, and one gilt cloth

holding a place in a story
one of us never quite saw to the end of.

Notre Père, Nos Poires

How spotted you are now, your skin
aspirin-bruised, flesh war-soft and weepy,

your Lucy all in pieces, you
still full of juice. On the dig site: dust.

Dust and flies and "Lucy in the Sky
with Diamonds." Vapor trails of passing

planes. Chisels and little brushes.
We offered you fruit, four goats, firstborn

sons, but you wanted only bowls
of cereal and touchstone quotes.

We offered you our fame that you might
taste it—winter pears on the highest

branches. I love a bruised fruit best
for how I eat around it, the way

the wind makes rock formations
out of lithified sand. Juice

on my chin, my fingers tacky
afterward. Carried across

continents, she comes together
again in the minds of the marvelous.

Our father, she gets up again,
she stands on two feet, she walks

without pain toward the orchard.

To Arms

Along the muddy banks of the inlet,
fiddler crabs scuttled into foaming holes,
the males with their major claws
snipping the air, their stalked eyes wild,
while my brothers and I, with tanned arms,
catapulted sea-polished stones at them.
When we returned to base at the tiny cape,
our grandmother's arm, scalded days before
by a dropped cauldron of tomato sauce,
had swelled to twice its size, third-degree burns
oozing pus and blood. Our mother, a nurse,
wound a dressing of fresh gauze.
I remember the old woman's soft moan,
her dark eyes shining. She had no hole
to crawl into, so she rocked in the breezeway,
with a view of the yard, the blue hydrangeas,
and the men on the chaises, their thick arms
bending as they brought the brown bottles
to their burned lips as if in victory.

Music from a Farther Room

The flute, the sackbut, the dulcimer
in the rooms of the dying. The harp,
the cornet, the psaltery. The look

of the eyes' last seeing when the ears
hear their final note or chord. The flats
some know as sharps. A bee batting a screen.

Thales of Crete appeased the wrath
of Apollo with paeans to end a plague,
and in all of Sparta's rooms,

close with death, that conclusive music.
But meadowlarks, too. Finches. Thrushes
in the distant woods. Birds which are

themselves flutes, sackbuts, dulcimers
dressed in feathers. Up in Amherst
Emily's last breath of the bobolink's

virtuosic bubbling. A mother's cooing,
half weeping, half exalted send-off
heard beyond a locked door. Anywhere

and often. In Pittsburgh the shrill whistle
of the steel mill; how many have ridden
that held note into infinity? In Treblinka

the shrill whistling trains, the chuff,
the cough, the high-note wail.
On the Oregon Trail the pioneer's wheel.

The ship's whistle for the immigrant
whose filmed eyes never did see Ellis Island.
The fading brain takes what it's offered.

My mother's mother, no instrument
but the clock ticking, the ice clinking
its melt in a bedside tumbler.

O, don't we each have our deaths set
to music? Natural or manmade. The tabla,
the tabor, the steam calliope.

Beethoven's "Moonlight Sonata" playing
tinny through headphones stuck
in someone else's busy ears. C# minor.

What do we hear there at the edge,
the threshold, the dark verge,
when sense, no more than a warm room,

echoes emptily? How must the bedside
cello sound, how the car horn, how
the human voice hushing us at the last?

If not so much the tension of the song
resolved, at least let it be the force
of the crossing when the humming ceases.

Acknowledgments

Grateful acknowledgment is made to the following publications in which these poems first appeared, sometimes in earlier versions:

The American Journal of Nursing: "Cordon Sanitaire"
The American Journal of Poetry: "Gray Water," "Husbandry," "Purgatory Chasm"
The Christian Science Monitor: "Garden Shed in Winter"
The Common: "Coronation"
Crazyhorse: "Notre Père, Nos Poires," "Toward the Far Shore"
Duende: "Because It Is Cold and Nightfall Comes"
Epoch: "Sensible Transfer," "To Arms"
Galway Review: "Moose in the Yard"
Green Linden: "Forgetfulness"
JuxtaProse: "A Flock of Starlin*gs*"
The Massachusetts Review: "Music from a Farther Room"
The New Criterion: "Shoring Up"
The New Yorker: "Making Love in the Kitchen," "Pretend It Was Just the Wind"
North American Review: "Horace, I Dream of Watches"
Pif Magazine: "The Falling Man," "Loons"
Ploughshares: "Wild Columbine"
Salamander: "Flying Saucers"
Shenandoah: "Heat Lightning," "Returning to Iowa"
Turtle Island Quarterly: "Destroying Angel"
Upstreet: "Driving All Night"

"Flying Saucers" was featured on *Poetry Daily* on August 19, 2016.

"Music from a Farther Room" was featured on *Poetry Daily* on January 12, 2017.

"Purgatory Chasm" was reprinted in the anthology *Even the Daybreak: 35 Years of Salmon Poetry* (Salmon Poetry, 2016).

"Making Love in the Kitchen" was translated into Italian and published in *Internazionale,* Rome, Italy in August, 2015.

"Music from a Farther Room" was chosen for the Anne Halley Poetry Prize by the editors of *The Massachusetts Review* and published as a limited edition broadside in 2017.

I would like to thank Blue Mountain Center and Marble House Project for residencies during which some of these poems were written.

About the Author

Gary J. Whitehead's third book of poetry, *A Glossary of Chickens,* was chosen by Paul Muldoon for the Princeton Series of Contemporary Poets and published in 2013 by Princeton University Press. His poems have appeared in such publications as *The New Yorker, Shenandoah,* and *Ploughshares.* His work has also been featured on *Poetry Daily, Verse Daily, The Guardian's Poem of the Week,* the BBC's *Words and Music* program, and *American Life in Poetry.* Awards for his poetry include the Anne Halley Prize from *The Massachusetts Review,* a New York Foundation for the Arts Fellowship, and the Pearl Hogrefe Fellowship at Iowa State University. He has been a featured poet at the Geraldine R. Dodge Poetry Festival, the Princeton Poetry Festival, and the West Caldwell Poetry Festival, and has held residencies at Blue Mountain Center, Mesa Refuge, the Heinrich Böll Cottage, and Marble House Project. He teaches English at Tenafly High School in New Jersey.

www.garyjwhitehead.com

CPSIA information can be obtained
at www.ICGtesting.com
Printed in the USA
BVHW071258070119
537203BV00014B/1664/P